Rockin' Crafts

Everything You Need to Become a Rock-Painting Craft Star!

Editor: Rebecca J. Razo
Art Direction: Shelley Baugh
Production Design: Debbie Aiken, Rae Siebels
Production Management: Irene Chan, Rushi Sanathra,
Nicole Szawlowski
Author and Crafter: Diana Fisher
Copyeditor: Meghan O' Dell
Publisher: Pauline Molinari

Designed and Published by Walter Foster Publishing, Inc.
3 Wrigley, Suite A
Irvine, CA 92618
www.walterfoster.com

Printed in China.

Table of Contents

Let's Rock!

Are you ready to rock? If so, you've come to the right place! This book reveals the secrets to the ultra-cool art of rock painting. Sure, people have been painting rocks for thousands of years (ever heard of cave paintings?), but you've never seen rock art like this before. Let's get started!

Gather Your Rockin' Supplies

Get ready to create your rock masterpieces by gathering the supplies shown below. You'll use a whole bunch of decorations—from feathers and glitter to beads and googly eyes!

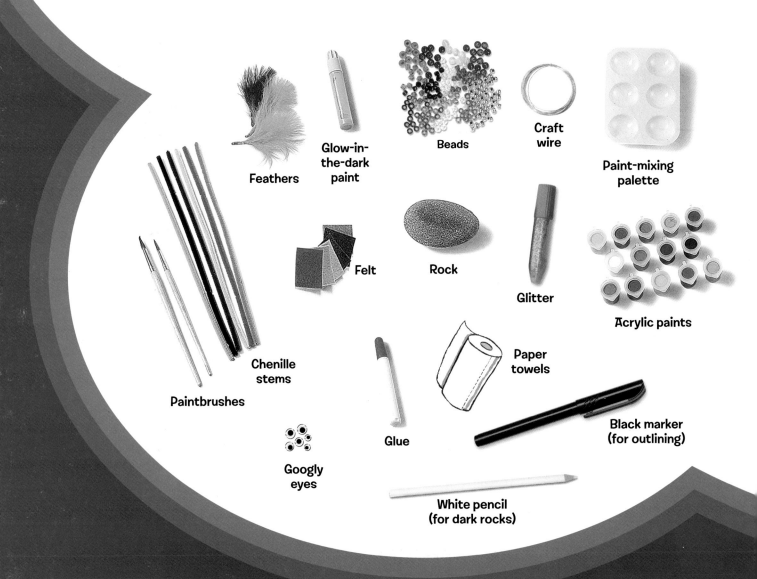

Feathers

Glow-in-the-dark paint

Beads

Craft wire

Paint-mixing palette

Paintbrushes

Chenille stems

Felt

Rock

Glitter

Acrylic paints

Googly eyes

Glue

Paper towels

Black marker (for outlining)

White pencil (for dark rocks)

Mixing it Up

Bring your rocks to life with these rockin' color combinations!

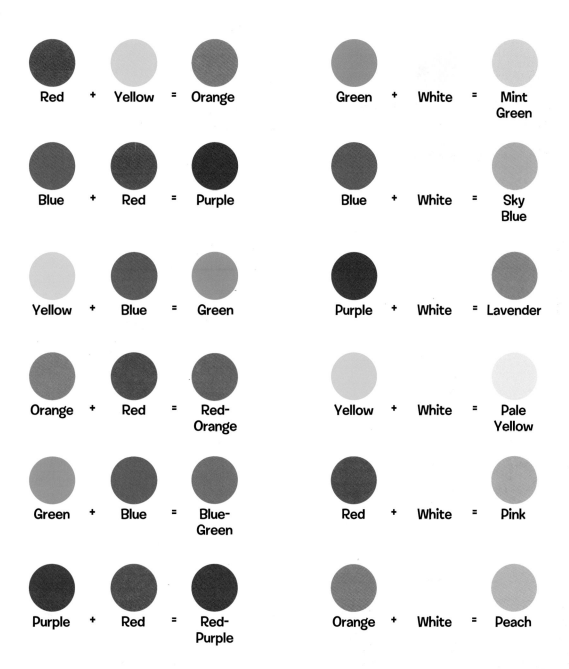

Red + Yellow = Orange

Green + White = Mint Green

Blue + Red = Purple

Blue + White = Sky Blue

Yellow + Blue = Green

Purple + White = Lavender

Orange + Red = Red-Orange

Yellow + White = Pale Yellow

Green + Blue = Blue-Green

Red + White = Pink

Purple + Red = Red-Purple

Orange + White = Peach

The Hunt Begins

Each Rock Is Unique

Whether you're on a hike or in your own backyard, every rock you find is special—it's *your* rock. And what's more, it's as unique as you are! Yep, that's right—your rock is 100% original; there's not another one in the world like it. So which project should you use your rock for? That all depends on your imagination! Take a moment and give your rock a good hard look—what does it look like to you? Is it shaped like a car? A bug? A spaceship? An egg? You decide. Use your rock for one of the many rockin' projects in this book or dream up your own project—it's all up to you. With a little paint (and a little imagination), you can transform your rock into anything you like!

The most important materials you'll need to begin painting rocks are, well, rocks! Hunting for the perfect sizes and shapes for your paintings is an adventure in itself! For smooth rocks, try exploring nearby creeks or streams. Or you can check out local hiking trails or fields for other kinds of natural rocks. You may even want to purchase your rocks—home and garden stores and nurseries often have a supply of stones for sale.

Rock Your World!

Use the patterns starting on page 56 to paint your own cool rocks.

Prep School

Before you start painting, you need to prepare your rocks. (In other words, you need to wash them!) Once you have a scrub brush in hand, all you need is water. Soak your rocks in a plastic tub or a bucket of water, or spray them with a garden hose. That's all there is to it—except for a few words of caution: Don't wash your rocks in the sink or bathtub because the rocks might scratch them.

Transferring a Design

1 First size your pattern so that it fits your rock, enlarging or reducing it with a printer or photocopier. Then completely cover the back of the design with pencil, pressing firmly. (Use black pencil for light rocks, white for dark.)

2 Now carefully cut along the outline of the design with a pair of scissors. If your rock isn't perfectly flat, cut out little triangles around the edge of the pattern. (This will help you tape the paper flat against the surface of the rock.)

3 Now use masking tape or artist's tape to attach the pattern to your clean rock. Be sure to place the tape over only the white parts of the design; you don't want to cover up the guidelines you'll be transferring to your rock.

4 Trace over the design with a ballpoint pen, pressing firmly. The pencil from the back of the design will transfer to the rock. When you are finished tracing, lift off the pattern. Your rock pencil sketch is ready!

Rock Bottom Basics

Once you've learned the basic painting techniques on these pages, you'll be ready to start rockin' around the clock!

Building Up Thin Colors

The colors shown above are very thin. To make sure the rock doesn't show through these colors, build up the color by applying several thin layers of paint. For the first layer, mix some white into the color to make it look thicker; when this dries, paint over this layer with the pure color.

Blending Colors Wet-on-Wet

Painting wet-on-wet is a cool way to blend colors without mixing them together. Apply the first color and wipe off the brush with a paper towel. While the paint is still wet, apply the second color, overlapping the first. Lightly brush the area where the colors meet to blend them.

Avoiding Wet Paint

To keep from smudging your fresh paint, try holding your rock in place with a toothpick instead of your fingers. Also place your rock on paper so you can rotate the paper instead of the rock. And always let one side of the rock dry completely before painting the other side.

Drybrushing on Texture

Drybrushing can add shading or texture to your rock art, making it extra cool and "professional" looking. First load a brush with paint. Then spread out the bristles by wiggling the brush on a paper towel. Wipe off the excess paint; then lightly brush the rock with short strokes.

Taking Shortcuts

A fine-tipped, permanent black marker is great for outlining designs on your rocks (instead of painting them). Just draw or transfer your design on the rock. Then use the marker to carefully trace over the pencil lines. Wait for the marker ink to dry and then add paint!

Drawing with Your Brush

It's easy to "draw" thin lines, letters, and details—just use a small brush! First add a little water to the paint to make it flow smoothly. Then load a small brush with a little paint (not too much, or you'll get blobs!). Hold the brush upright and "draw" with the tip.

Spotting Painting Tools

A cotton swab makes a fun painting tool! Use it to dot on tiny circles, like a ladybug's spots. Other household items can become painting tools too. For example, try painting with a sponge, a rag, or even an old toothbrush to create unique shapes and textures on your rocks.

Practicing Patience

Sure, it's important to learn how to mix colors or use different application techniques, but the most important artistic skill you can learn is patience! Painting lines slowly, taking time to wait for layers to dry, and carefully mixing colors will result in truly amazing rock masterpieces!

Animals Rock!

Rock-a-Bye Puppy

This pup makes a great doorstop because he sleeps like a rock! Just set him down and he'll do his job without bark or sigh!

Puppy

1

Choose a large oval rock. Sketch the dog design with a pencil (or transfer the pattern); then trace over the design with a small brush and black paint. You can also use a permanent marker.

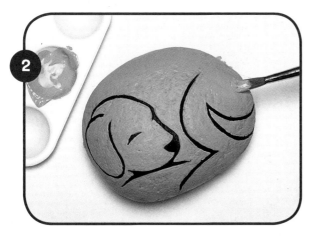

2

Now paint the dog with a golden yellow, working around the outline so that most of the black lines are left showing. Remember to paint down along the sides of the rock.

3

After the paint dries, mix a little white into your golden color. Then paint the hairs, making short, thin strokes with the tip of a small brush. Finally, add a pink highlight on the nose.

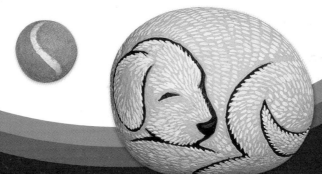

Pet Rocks

What could be more purr-fect than pet rocks? They're low-care, low-cost pets that can be yours for only pebbles a day!

Cat

1 Choose a round, flat rock and paint both sides white. (Remember to let the paint dry on one side before turning it over!) When the white has dried, paint the entire rock yellow.

2 When the yellow paint is dry, transfer the pattern or use it as a guideline. Then add groups of three orange "tabby" stripes along the top and sides of the rock.

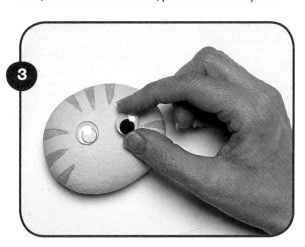

3 Now position and glue on the eyes. You can place them close together or far apart, but remember to leave enough room below the eyes for the nose and mouth.

4 Paint the black outlines of the nose and the mouth with a small brush. Then use the tip of the brush to paint black whiskers. When the black is completely dry, fill in the nose with pink.

12

5

Cut out triangles of yellow and pink felt for the ears. Glue the smaller pink triangles on top of the yellow ones; then glue the ears to the back of the cat's head.

Choose a small, flat-bottomed rock to paint green. Glue on eyes, paint the mouth and legs, and dot on yellow with a cotton swab. Cut out green felt feet and glue them to the bottom.

Mouse

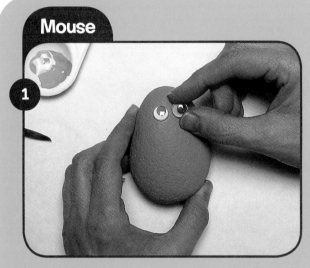

1

Apply gray paint to both sides of an oval, flat-bottomed rock. (To make gray, mix a little white into black.) When the paint is dry, glue on the eyes.

2

Use a small brush to outline the nose and to add the mouth and whiskers. When the paint is dry, fill in the nose with pink. (For a darker pink, mix more red into the white.)

3

Cut out felt ear and feet shapes. Glue the pink teardrops on the gray domes. Pinch and glue the ears closed; then glue them to the back of the head. Glue the feet to the base of the rock.

4

Wrap a pink chenille stem around a pencil to make it curly. (Or bunch it up for a scraggly tail.) Then glue the chenille to the back of the rock to finish your mouse-terpiece!

13

Rocks of a Feather

They may be birdbrains, but this flock of feathered friends has enough smarts to be "cuckoo" about rock painting!

Ostrich

First paint a smooth, oval rock black. Then fold a chenille stem in half and twist the ends together. At the tips, glue on eyes and a feather.

Glue the neck to the rock; add feathers for wings and felt for the beak. Next crimp two pieces of chenille as shown above to make legs with toes; then glue these to the rock.

Chicken

Begin by painting an oval rock white. Paint the beak and feet brown; when they're dry, paint all but the edges orange.

After the orange paint is dry, glue on googly eyes, placing them just above the beak.

Now glue three feathers to the back of the bird's body to create wings and a headdress.

Imagination Rocks!

The Sword and the Stone

Want to create fantastic fire-breathing dragons, towering fortresses, and powerful wizards? You won't need a magic wand—just grab a paintbrush!

Wizard

1 Choose a tall, somewhat triangular rock with a flat bottom (so that it can stand upright). Transfer the design to the rock with a pencil; then outline it with black paint. Paint the wizard's robe, hat, face, and beard.

2 After the first coats of paint dry, you're ready for the details. Dot on the wizard's eyes with black paint. Mix a dark gray; then use this color to paint bushy eyebrows and a thick, droopy mustache.

3 Now paint the eyebrows and mustache white, but be sure to leave a little dark gray outline. Use a small brush to decorate the robe with yellow moons and golden yellow stars.

Dragon

1

Start with a large oval rock. Transfer the dragon pattern to the rock. Then trace over the design with black paint, using the tip of your paintbrush to "draw" the fine lines.

2

Cover the dragon's body with the green paint, working around the black outlines. Use a darker green (add black) to fill in the spiky plates along the back and tail.

3

Use the tip of the brush and the same darker green that you used for the plates to paint curlicues on the dragon's knee and elbow, make half-circles for the scales, and add an eyebrow.

4

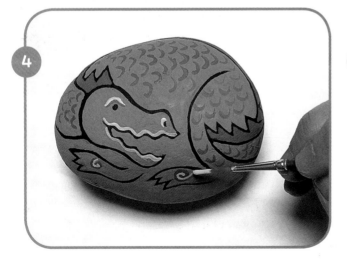

Rinse your brush and switch to yellow paint to add a highlight to both the curlicues and the eyebrow. Then outline the nostril and mouth.

5

Paint the dragon's flames with red and yellow. Then cut out felt wings. Cut a piece of craft wire and shape it to match the top edge of the wing; then glue it to the felt. When the paint and the glue are both dry, glue the wings onto the rock.

Castle

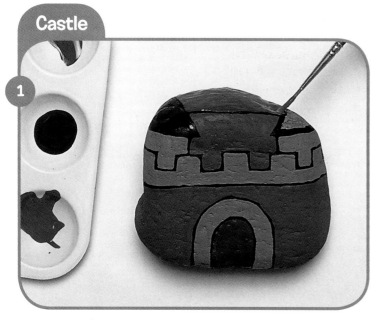

Transfer the castle design to a square rock. Then paint the castle with two shades of gray (mixes of black with white). Use brown for the drawbridge and the tops of the towers; then paint the top of the castle purple.

Mix two shades of lighter gray by adding more white to the grays from step 1. With the lightest gray, paint stone blocks across the top of the wall and around the drawbridge. With the other gray, add scattered blocks on the castle wall.

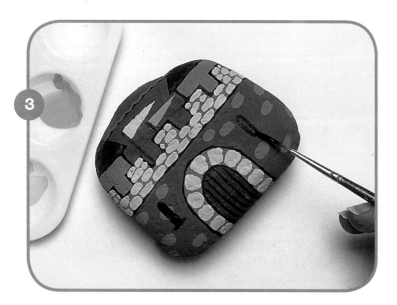

Add more white to the purple to highlight the top edge; then add colorful flags. Paint black lines on the drawbridge door for planks of wood, and use a small brush to add thin black windows on the walls.

Don't Rock the Boat

Sailors, beware! There be pirates in these waters, after yer shiny rocks. (Them be jewels and nuggets of gold!)

Turn a few pebbles into pirates' riches with a coat of yellow paint! Add ¢ and $ symbols in brown; then cover your nuggets with gold glitter glue to make them sparkle.

Pirate

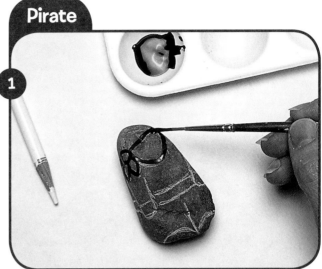

1

On a thin, oval rock, transfer the pirate's pattern. Use a white pencil if your rock is very dark. Then go over the lines with black paint and a small brush.

Pirate Ship

1

For the ship, choose a rock that's not entirely symmetrical. Transfer the ship design with pencil; then outline it with black paint. Next paint thick black lines for the spaces between the sails.

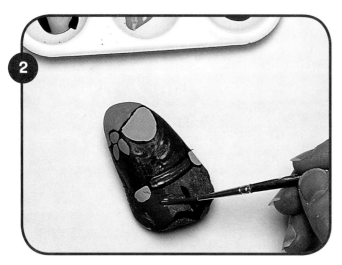

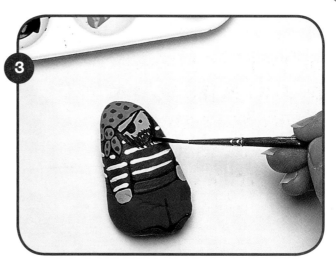

Begin filling in the color, painting inside the black outlines. Use bright green for the pirate's bandana, red for the shirt, brown for the belt, and blue for the pants, with a bit of peach for the skin.

Now finish the details. Paint blue polka dots on the bandana and white stripes on the shirt. Then add an eye, an eye patch, and a scraggly beard (use short, vertical strokes). "Arrr!"

Now use white paint to fill in the sails, leaving the black lines showing between them. Paint the ship's hull dark brown with red trim and add black between the hull and sails.

With a lighter brown (add a little white to the brown), paint thin lines for wooden planks on the hull. With a small brush and a little black, draw a skull and crossbones on the sail.

Treasure Chest

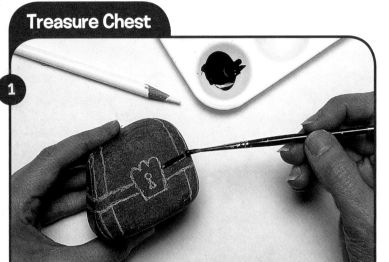

Cube-shaped rocks make good treasure chests. First transfer the pattern to the rock (or draw freehand if you like). Next outline the drawing with black paint and a small brush.

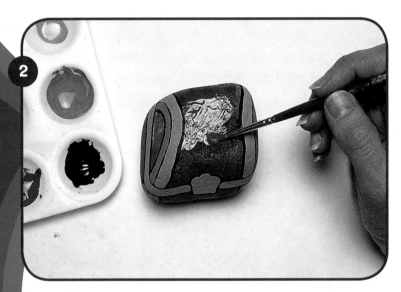

When the black outlines have dried, fill in the "metal" bands and lock using gray paint. Then paint the wood brown, leaving the black outline of the metal bands showing.

Next paint horizontal black lines to create the wood boards; use light brown strokes for the grain. Paint a keyhole on the lock and add dark gray dots for the nails.

Rockville

People have been building towns with stones for ages. With this project, you can create your own village, rock-full of your favorite shops and stops!

Car

1 Oval rocks with flat bottoms make great cars! First transfer the pattern to the rock. Use black paint to outline the design, fill in the windows and tires, and paint the bottom of the car.

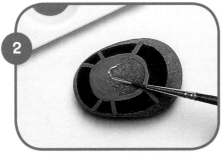

2 Now paint the top and the body of the car. Use the tip of a small brush to carefully paint the thin lines between the windows; it's okay if you slightly overlap the black windows.

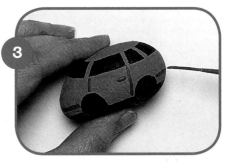

3 Mix a darker color (add a little black to the body color); then paint the details. Use the tip of a small brush to paint lines for the front and back bumpers, the doors, and the handles.

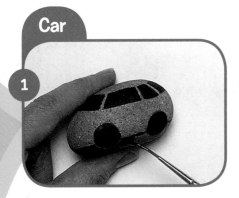

4 Now paint two yellow headlights just above the front bumper line and two red taillights just above the back bumper line. Next add a white highlight to the door handle.

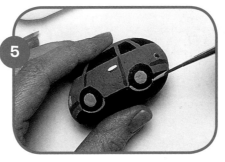

5 Mix some light gray paint for the round wheels of each tire. Then, using the tip of a small brush, apply a thin line of gray under each tire, highlighting the edge. (This gives the tires dimension.)

6 Next paint the wheel design, using an X or three lines (as shown here). You can also add more details to your stone vehicle, such as a license plate or a hood ornament.

Post Office

1 For this post office, sketch the design on a square rock. Then paint over the lines and fill in the windows with black. Next paint the roof red and the walls light blue.

2 Now paint a series of scallops on the roof, starting at the peak and working down. Add a white line around each window with the tip of the brush; then paint the inside of the door white.

3 Next use a small brush to add details. You can paint a name or add features like the flowers at the base of this post office. And you can even add items in the windows of your store!

Rock-et into Outer Space

Get ready to blast off on an out-of-this-world adventure, complete with rocket ships and UFOs. If you'd love to get within a stone's throw of an alien, this project is for you!

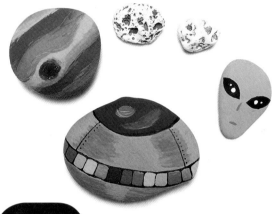

Asteroid

Rough, pitted rocks make great moons and asteroids—all you have to do is paint them white! For deeper-looking pits, leave the holes unpainted.

Planet

For the planet, cover a round rock with stripes. Begin with a wavy line of color. Then paint wet-on-wet: Wipe off the brush and overlap the next color while the paint is still wet.

Alien

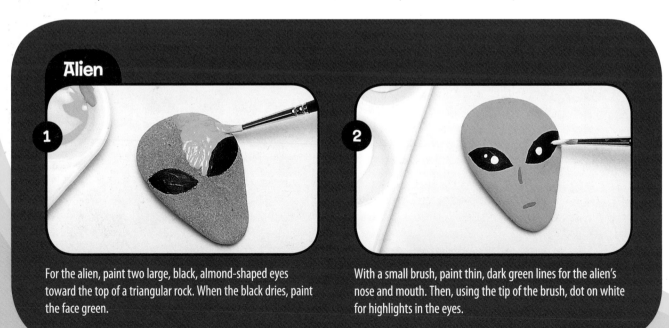

1 For the alien, paint two large, black, almond-shaped eyes toward the top of a triangular rock. When the black dries, paint the face green.

2 With a small brush, paint thin, dark green lines for the alien's nose and mouth. Then, using the tip of the brush, dot on white for highlights in the eyes.

Flying Saucer

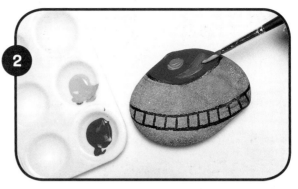

1 Apply gray paint to both sides of an oval, flat-bottomed rock. (To make gray, mix a little white into black.) Then, when the paint is dry, glue on the eyes.

2 Apply dark blue to the dome. Then, painting wet-on-wet (see page 8), brush on light blue highlights. To blend, stroke only a few times so the highlight still shows.

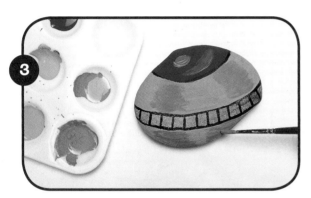

3 Cover the ship's body with a coat of gray paint. Then, while the gray is still wet, brush on blue and purple shadows using short strokes. Remember not to blend too much.

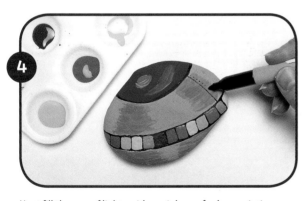

4 Next fill the row of lights with a rainbow of colors, painting inside the black outlines. When the paint is completely dry, paint or draw the black seam and bolt details.

Rock Garden

You'll never be "bugged" to water these flowers!

Butterfly

Select a rock with a squarish shape and transfer the pattern to the front. Then paint black lines over your sketch and fill in the empty spaces with black.

Now paint the wings, starting with the darkest colors. Let each color dry before adding the next. Because the orange paint is very thin, apply a layer of white first.

When the first coat of paint is completely dry, paint the butterfly's body. Use a small brush to dot on light blue around the butterfly's wings; then paint yellow on top of the orange.

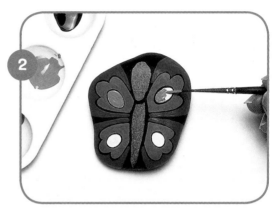

Now twist craft wire around a pencil or crimp it to make the antennae. Glue the antennae to the back of the butterfly, resting them on another rock to keep them in position as they dry.

When the glue has dried completely, turn over the butterfly. Position two googly eyes on the head. (You might want to try different sizes.) When you're pleased with the size and placement, glue the eyes to the rock.

Daisies

For a garden of daisies, paint an oval rock dark green. Then paint leaves with medium green, letting some of the dark green show through. Paint blue petals with a small brush. Then dot on yellow centers with the brush tip.

Red Flower

For this flower, choose a round, flat rock. Sketch your design; then paint over the pencil lines with black. When the paint dries, add the red petals and the orange center. Then add yellow dots to the center and brown lines for the petal detail.

Rosebud

On a flat, triangular rock, first draw the zigzag base design and two lines for the petals. Then paint the green base and pink petals; use a darker green to paint lines on the base. Mix a little white with the pink for the final highlights.

Hobbies Rock!

We Will Rock You!

These stones sport serious team spirit! Cheer on your favorite sports and teams with these awesome athletic paperweights.

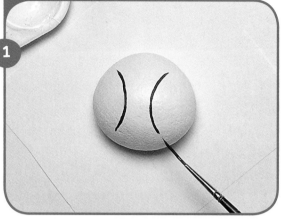

1

First paint both sides of a round rock white. When it's dry, add two red curved lines, as shown.

2

On the back of the ball, paint two of the same red curves, and connect the lines on the sides, as shown.

3

Let the paint dry completely. Then paint short stitches across the red lines with the tip of a small brush.

Baseball Glove

Paint a flat, square rock with a mix of orange and brown. Then add the design in black, including the stitching detail.

Football

Choose an oval rock with pointed ends and paint it reddish-brown. When the paint dries, add white stripes, a seam, and stitches.

Rockin' Royalty

Ready to battle your way through a rocky game of chess? If not, the pawns are always happy to play a game of checkers instead!

Pawns

For pawns, you'll need 16 small rocks (use 24 rocks for checkers). Paint 8 rocks one color and the other 8 rocks another color. When they are dry, add faces.

Queen

1

Find similarly shaped, flat-bottomed rocks for the kings, queens, rooks, and bishops. Draw each design; then paint over the lines with black.

2

Now paint the fronts of the rocks. Choose one color group, such as blue or red, for each army. When the front dries, paint the back too.

Knight

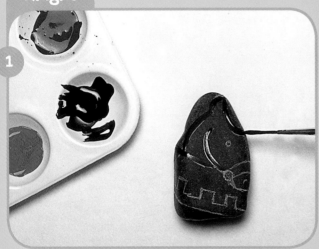

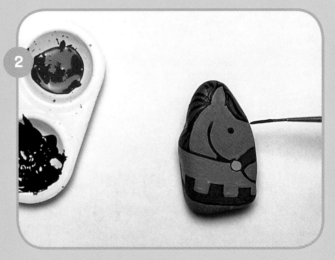

Find triangular rocks for the knights (a knight is a horse). Draw the design, outline it in black, and paint the black lines of the mane. Repeat on the back.

Now paint the horse itself any color you like—it could even be green! Match the knight's armor to the queen's color scheme.

Rockin' Cats & Dogs

Since Fido and Fifi occupy a special place in your heart, why not honor each of them with their own personalized rocks?

Dog House

1 Start with a house-shaped rock to make your dog a rock star. Trim your picture to fit; then glue it on.

2 With black paint, outline the photo and the edge of the roof. Then paint the walls and roof.

3 Trim the roof with light brown and the door frame with white. Then decorate your doghouse! Woof!

1

2

For a rock with purr-sonality, include all your furry friends! On a large oval rock, paint wet-on-wet; apply one color after the next without blending.

Continue adding colors wet-on-wet until the rock is completely covered, blending a little to spread the paint into the empty areas.

3

4

When the paint is completely dry, cut your pictures into fun shapes, such as hearts, and then glue them to the flat part of the rock.

When the glue is dry, outline the pictures with glue and glitter (or use a glitter-glue pen). Ta-da!

Family Rocks

Picture yourself a rock star. Glue a picture of yourself to a rock, glitz it up, and—presto—you're ready to rock!

1 First find a flat rock and a photo that you would like to frame. Trim the photo to fit the rock, if necessary. Glue down the pic; then outline it with glue and glitter (or use a glitter-glue pen).

2 When the glue dries, brush paint between the two lines of glitter. While the paint is wet, sprinkle on beads. Then continue around the border, painting and sprinkling one section at a time.

3 Next paint a colorful design around the border, continuing down the sides of the rock. The bright, squiggly lines painted on this rock match the colors of the beads for a coordinated look!

36

Rock-Solid Friendships

A personalized decorative rock makes an ultra-original gift! Write a friend's name on the front of a rock or include a secret message on the back. On the flip side, experiment with one-of-a-kind colors and designs!

Message

Load your smallest brush with thin, white paint and use the tip to "write" your message on a flat rock of any shape. Then paint a design around the edges, continuing down the sides of the rock.

Name

1

Start with a colored oval on a flat, oval rock. When the paint dries, add the name. Paint thin black lines along the letters for shadows.

2

Now transfer the frame pattern to the rock or create your own design, using colorful lines, shapes, stripes—whatever you like!

3

Continue painting all the way down the sides of the rock, and always let the first layers of paint dry before moving on to the next colors.

Flip Side

Once your name or message is dry, flip over the rock to paint a colorful design on the opposite side. (For the name rock, this will be the back; for the message, the front.) Let each coat of paint dry before adding the next.

Funky Rocks!

Feed Your Rock Obsession

Everyone will think your parties rock with yummy foods on display!

Pizza

1. Choose a flat, triangular rock for the pizza. Transfer the pepperoni pizza pattern to the rock, or draw your own creation. Then paint the lines with black.

2. Now paint the sauce red, the cheese white, and the pepperoni reddish-brown. For the crust, mix white with a little brown, adding more brown for the darker edge.

3. When the paint has dried, add the details. Paint yellow highlights on the cheese and add tiny black Xs on the pepperoni slices to create spots of pepper.

Candy

1 For a box of candy, begin with a black square near the center of the rock. When this dries, paint brightly colored circles over the black.

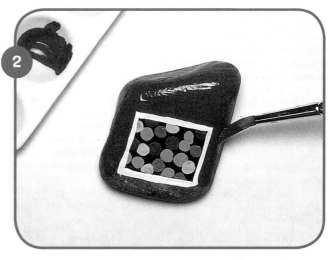

2 Now paint the box, starting with a white outline around the "window." When the front of the box is dry, turn the rock over to paint the back.

3 Now thin some white paint with water and brush a few highlights across the window. Finish by painting the name of your candy.

Hot Dog

1

Choose a long, oval rock for the hot dog (or "veggie" dog). Draw the bun shape, making it a bit shorter than the hot dog. You can draw the bun as two separate ovals on each side, or make the bun with two sides that meet at the bottom.

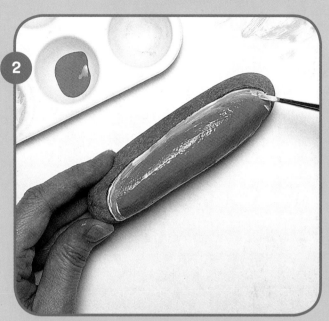

2

Mix white and brown to make the bun color; then paint one side of the bun. While the paint is wet, brush in a little white along the edge, using the wet-on-wet technique. Then paint the other side of the bun the same way.

3

When the bun color is completely dry, apply a black outline along the edge of the bun. Then mix a tiny bit of brown or black with red for a realistic meat color. Use this color to paint the hot dog, slightly over-lapping the black outline.

4

Next paint a thick yellow squiggle of mustard on top. (For a bright yellow, you may need more than one coat of paint.) Your party foods are ready—bring on the guests!

Rock Idols

Sure, they may have once been guardians of the tropical islands, but now these tikis work for you— as guardians of your books!

Tiki Bookend

1

Choose a heavy rectangular rock. Sketch the design with pencil; then paint over the lines with black.

2

Fill in the mouth with black. Then add brown for the tiki wood, including the eyes, nose, cheeks, and top of the head. Lighten the brown with white to paint lines for the wood grain.

3

Now paint the face, adding white to each color to create more contrast against the dark wood. Let the paint dry between coats.

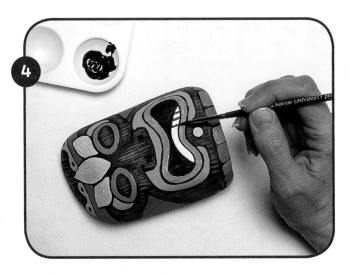

4

Next add the details, such as the dot on the chin and the stripes at the base. With a small brush, paint thin black lines for the teeth.

5

To prevent your tiki bookend from scratching your furniture, cut out a small piece of felt and glue it to the bottom of the rock.

43

Holidays Rock!

United We Rock

What do you get when you bring stars, stripes, and stones together? Perfectly patriotic rocks! With these paperweights, you can celebrate America all year long.

Patriotic Star

For a creative patriotic piece, draw a five-point star on a round, flat rock. Paint the bottom of the star white. When the white is dry, add red stripes over the white and let them dry.

Now paint the top of the star blue. Keep the line above the red-and-white striped area nice and straight, but don't worry if you paint outside of the star lines; the next color will cover that up.

When the paint is dry, mix white and blue to make a sky blue. Then fill in the background of the rock by carefully painting this color around the outline of the star.

State Silhouette

First choose a rock that fits your state's shape. Draw the outline of the state, leaving room for the name; then go over the sketch with black.

Now paint the background. (You might choose your state's colors for the design.) After the background dries, paint the state.

After working out the placement of the letters, pencil on the state name. Outline it in black using a marker or paint.

American Flag

To make a U.S. flag on a rectangular rock, draw the "stars" square, painting everything around it white. When the paint dries, add red stripes (four next to the stars square and three below).

Now paint the square dark blue. When the paint is dry, use the tip of a small brush to dot on white stars. Alternate between rows of six stars and rows of five until you have nine rows.

47

Egg-ceptional Rocks

Nothing says spring like a basket full of . . . stones! And these colorful rock creations are perfect for egg hunts—they aren't as fragile as eggs, and they never spoil.

Daisy Egg

1

First sketch the design all the way around an oval or egg-shaped rock; then use straight, scalloped, zigzagged, and squiggly lines to separate the color sections.

1

For a different egg rock design, start by painting the entire rock with one color. Bright colors, like yellow, will stand out best. Remember to let the front of the rock dry completely before painting the back.

2

Now paint the sections with your favorite spring colors. To make pastel colors, just add a little white to any color (see "Mixing it Up" on page 5 for color combinations). When this layer dries, decorate the egg with polka dots or flowers.

2

When the base coat dries, use your small brush to paint squiggles, swirls, hearts, flowers, or anything else you like. You can also write names or messages—such as "Happy Spring!"

Hearts of Stone

Valentine's Day is the perfect holiday for sharing your love of rock painting!

You'll be amazed at how many pebbles you can find that are shaped like hearts. You can decorate your hearts with Valentine messages. Or you can create a whole group of "candy hearts" with heart-felt sayings!

Grave Stones

If creepy crafts rock your world, you'll love these spooky ghosts, scary skulls, wicked witches, and eerie eyeballs!

For a scary glow-in-the-dark skull, begin with an oval- or light-bulb-shaped rock. Paint the entire rock with a coat of white paint.

When the coat of white paint has dried completely, paint over the entire skull with a layer of glow-in-the-dark green paint.

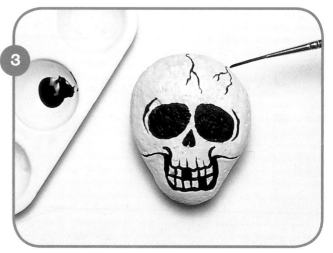

Now sketch the skull design. With black paint, outline the sketch and fill in the eye, nose, and teeth holes. Add cracks with the brush tip.

Bloodshot Eyeball

Begin with a round rock. (It doesn't have to be a perfect shape. Bumps will give it more gross-out appeal!) Paint the rock white. When dry, draw a circle and outline it with dark paint.

Next fill the inside of the circle with a green that is lighter than the color of the outline. When the paint is completely dry, brush a layer of glow-in-the-dark paint over the entire eyeball.

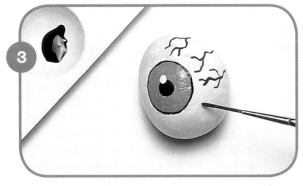

When the glow-in-the-dark paint is dry, color in the pupil with black paint, placing a white dot at the edge for a highlight; then paint wiggly red veins with the tip of a small brush.

Spider

For a spider, paint a round rock black and add a zigzag red mouth with pointy teeth. Then glue on eyes and 8 chenille stem legs. When the glue has dried, fold the legs.

Hanukkah Rocks

Star of David

1

Start with a flat, round rock. Then draw the Star of David by sketching two overlapping triangles in pencil—one pointing up, the other pointing down.

Menorah

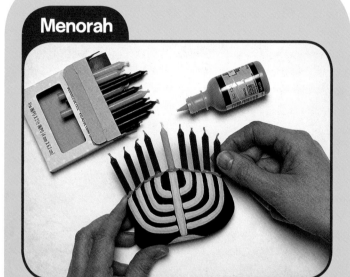

Sketch the center column, eight branches, and a base. Fill the background with black; then paint the menorah. When the paint dries, dot glue (or puffy paint) on top of each branch. When this is almost dry, add nine candles.

2

Now use a small brush to outline the pencil sketch with black paint. (It's okay if some pencil lines still show because you'll be painting over these areas in step 3.)

3

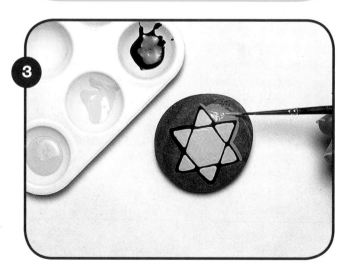

Paint the star one section at a time, slightly overlapping the black outlines. Finish by painting the background; start by carefully outlining the star's edges with a light blue color and then fill in the remainder of the rock.

Rockin' Patterns

Animals

Cat

Turtle

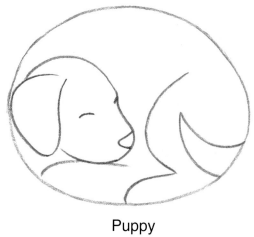

Puppy

Dragon & Castle

Castle

Wizard

Unicorn

Dragon

Pirates

Pirate

Pirate captain

Treasure chest

Pirate ship

Rockville

House front

House side

Car side

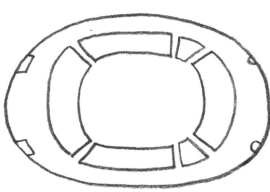

Car top

58

Outer Space

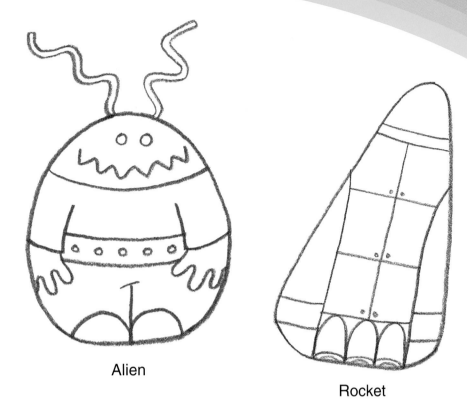

Alien

Rocket

Garden

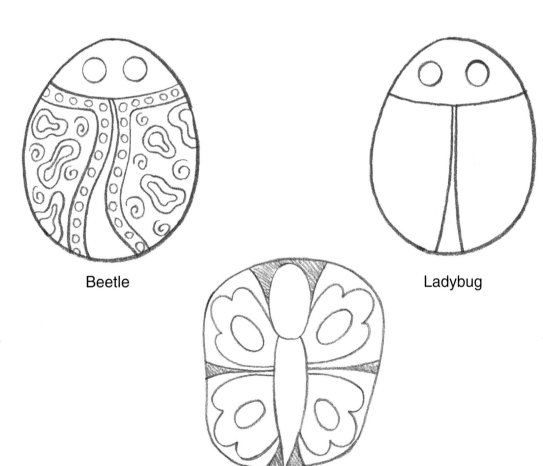

Beetle

Ladybug

Butterfly side

Butterfly front

59

Chess Set

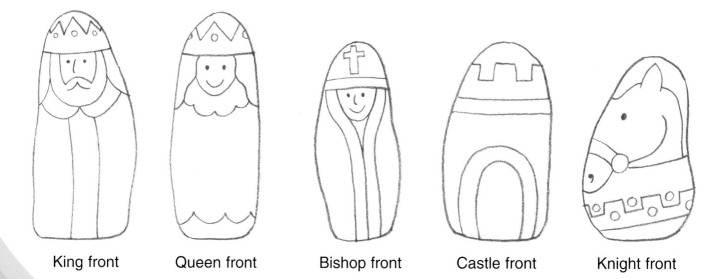

King front   Queen front   Bishop front   Castle front   Knight front

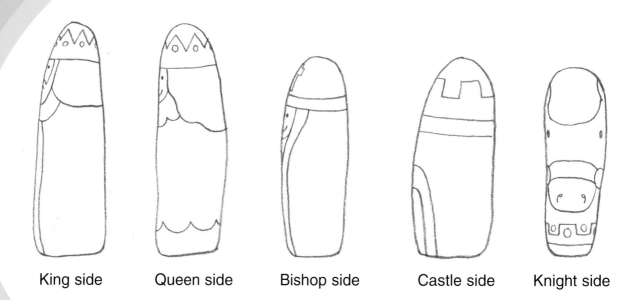

King side   Queen side   Bishop side   Castle side   Knight side

Friendship

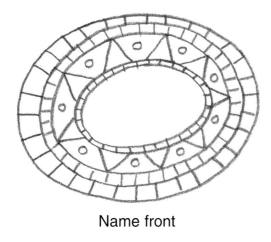

Name front

Message flip side

Food

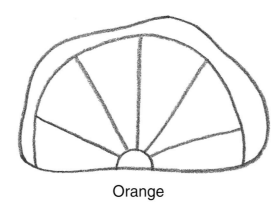

Orange

Bookends

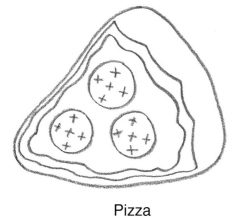

Pizza

Strawberry

Tiki

Holidays

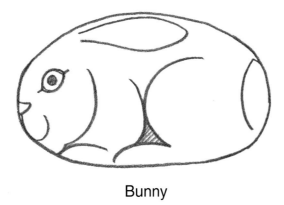

Bunny

Chick

Skull

Witch

62

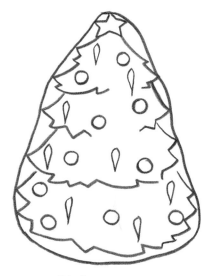

Christmas tree

Jack-o-Lantern

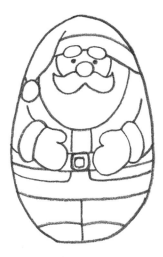

Santa

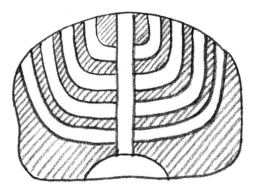

Menorah

Diana Fisher is an award-winning artist, author, and illustrator. Diana began winning awards and scholarships with her pencil, oil, and acrylic paintings and portraits while she was still in school. She then went on to study art in New York and computer graphics in Arizona. During her early career in advertising, Diana was recognized as one of the top illustrators in the southwest United States and later received accolades as a children's book illustrator.

Today, Diana continues to illustrate children's materials and design toys. She explores a variety of creative pursuits in both art and writing. Her studio is in the Arizona desert, where stark beauty and diverse wildlife make an inspirational backdrop for all forms of creativity.